AS A THANK YOU GIFT FOR PURCHASING

THE H.O.W. BOOK, GET THE

COMPANION WORKBOOK
(Printable pdf) FOR FREE!

GO HERE TO DOWNLOAD:

https://how.ck.page/c8d52ccf7e

Other books by Tralyne D. Usry
Aesthetically Audibly Me

Sweet Jambalaya

When Design Speaks

Nebby

H.O.W. Workbook

H.O.W.

How Overcomers Win

Written by Tralyne D. Usry
Edited by Jan Ham

Table of Contents

Table of Contents (Continued)

Dedication

This book is dedicated to my Aunt Donaval, a chosen, and dedicated woman of God without whom I would not have made it this far! Your sacrifices of love and care moved me to continue to pursue my dreams despite life's challenges. You are my constant reminder and implementor of

H.O.P.E.
(Heaven's Ordained Perfected Expectation)!

This work is also dedicated to my sister, Tajuana, better known as T.J. You, too, have sacrificed to attend to my every need and even my wants! You encouraged me to believe and trust in God regardless. You are my pillar of strength and security.

You two helped me to live!
YOU pushed THIS OVERCOMER TO WIN!
YOU helped me to learn **H.O.W.**!

Preface

What has happened to me? How did I get here? I can't walk. I can't go to the bathroom properly. I can't drive. I can't cook. I can't prepare my food. I can't take care of myself! What good am I to myself? To anyone? I am useless! I want out!

I spent months going back and forth to the doctor. The diagnosis, multiple sclerosis, was incurable and, for some, terminal (or fatal).

The thoughts that went through my head were all over the place. Will I ever walk again? Will I eventually need someone to take over my complete hygiene, bathing me, taking me to the bathroom, diapering me? Will I ever be able to teach again? Would I be dependent on someone for everything? Will I ever be employed again and, if so, doing what? Will I be able to do anything?

I wasn't smiling anymore. That bright, bubbly, optimistic girl was nowhere in sight! I didn't want to read my Bible. I didn't want to pray.

I questioned God. How could He have let this happen? I gave my life to Him at a young age, 18, and I served Him wholeheartedly for over 20 years. How God? Why God? Was He disappointed in me? Had I sinned and opened the door for this attack?

I know that I'm not alone. Others have had the same questions and more that desperately need answers. Life's challenges are numerous and ever present. There must be a way out. Ask me H.O.W.!

Foreword

Norfolk, Virginia
August 14, 2020

Chance meeting? I think not. Divinely set-up? Of course. I met Tralyne Usry over 15 years ago at a church where I was a member. Graduate school brought her to my hometown, but the Lord brought her into my life. From the moment our paths crossed, I was, immediately, in awe of her. She was younger than me but had a maturity and a love for God that I hadn't seen nor experienced before in someone her age. I knew from then on, our lives would forever be intertwined.

I have been exposed to her calling and giftings as Teacher of the Gospel, Spoken-Word Artist, Dancer, Screen Writer and Author. I've watched her, over the years, face, encounter, experience, tackle, and fight the challenges, events, and obstacles life would bring with a tenacity and warrior mentality. Through those challenges faced over the years, she gained the tools and insight necessary to overcome whatever stood in the way.

What better time than now when she again puts pen to paper and this time releases her memoir, her life's story about how she overcame, how she won the battles in her life. Who better to tell it than Tralyne, even in the midst of which probably is the biggest fight of her life (fighting Multiple Sclerosis) and winning! If you have faced, are facing or in the future will face - trust me, I'm sure you will - a challenge, fight, or battle, whether big or small, I admonish you to open your heart and mind to be inspired, encouraged, edified, and equipped to learn **How Overcomers Win!!!**

Crystal D. James

Chapter 1

Introduction

You are THE wonderfully and fearfully made creation of God! DO YOU KNOW WHAT THAT MEANS? God reverenced (deeply respect, high regard) you when He created you and He created you for a specific reason, to be His dwelling place. He desires to live in you! **I Corinthians 3:16 says so!** "Don't you know that you yourselves are God's **temple** and that God's Spirit dwells in your midst."

God, from the beginning, dwelled in Heaven. He and the angels were the only inhabitants. Satan got beside himself and created an uprising in Heaven that caused him and his "cronies" to be evicted.

Your temple is under attack regularly because the enemy is upset with you! He has been displaced from his dwelling place with God. Talk about a "turf war!" Every challenge you face can be traced back to his desire to destroy God's new dwelling place, YOU! He, Satan, can no longer return to the old one.

The attacks on your temple are intended to, by any means necessary, cause your house to fall, to be demolished into nothing but rubble. He attacks your confidence. "Confidence" is a part of your makeup, your foundation. If you disrupt the foundation of a house, the house will be unstable and eventually fall. He attacks your finances. Finances are stabilizers and sustainers, like beams and loadbearing walls. Without those, the walls or the roof cave in. The house is destroyed.

 This book will take you through some of my life's battles where the goal of the enemy was to destroy this house, the very essence of who I am but I overcame EVERY TIME! I WON!

Are you ready to win? Are you ready to overcome? Ask me

Mentoring Moment

You are embarking on a journey to rebuild or erect your house, YOU, to overcome the enemy that has fought to destroy you from the beginning. Enough is enough!

These mentoring moments are designed to help you develop the skills to overcome or to help someone else to overcome. To do so, we will **E.D.I.F.Y.!**

The word "**edify**" comes from the Latin word "aedificare" which is a verb that means to erect a house. We will **E.D.I.F.Y.** to OVERCOME!

E.VALUATE

D.ISMANTLE

I.NVEST

F.ORTIFY

Y.IELD

Remember, you are the temple (I Corinthians 3:16), dwelling place, the HOUSE of God! Whenever life's challenges come, the enemy tries to make you believe that you won't make it. You will be overtaken or defeated by "this one!" Remember this fact also. "THE DEVIL IS A LIAR" (John 8:44b)!

Anything he says, know that the opposite is true! When he says, "You'll always be broke," you should say, "Oh, thank you for reassuring me that my financial situation has improved." When he says, "You'll always be depressed," you should say, "Oh, I'm healed and have joy every single day. Thanks for reassuring me!" Those words are weapons hurled at you to destroy you, cause cracks in your foundation, holes in your walls, and instability in your structure. You can do this!

Chapter 2

Letters of the Alphabet

I sat in that exam room waiting for the news. Disinfectant and sterilization filled my nostrils as the hands on the wall clock ticked loudly. What is taking this doctor so long? It was already what felt like an eternity since I'd been subjected to countless magnetic resonance imaging (MRI) tests and now more waiting? Torture!

"Good morning," said the Croatian thick-accented figure that came through the door. She extended her hand to greet me. I didn't even want to be in that room. So, I wasn't much for pleasantries, but my momma taught me better, so I obliged her. My aunt greeted this enemy with a smile.

She introduced herself and sat down in front of the computer. She shuffled some papers around on the desk and began to talk about what was on her computer screen. Her accent was so pronounced that most of her words sounded like they weren't in English. She talked and talked and talked. She pointed to things on the computer that looked as foreign as she sounded.

After what seemed like an eternity, she started to explain drug options. She said the name of the first one and started to list side effects, I stopped her mid-sentence. "You're talking about drugs I can take but you haven't told me what I have?" I emphatically stated. My aunt spoke up. "She said you have MS." The letters "MS" began to repeat in my head. It was as if it was playing on a scratched record and the needle was stuck. MS! MS! MS!

I'd obviously missed her saying it through her initial dissertation. There was some English spoken. Who knew?

I had to regain focus and come back to the conversation especially since it was about me.

She continued to discuss medication options ... each one with horrible side effects. PML! More letters! These letters started a barrage of terrifying thoughts. Progressive Multifocal Leukoencephalopathy (PML) is a fatal brain infection that was a possible side effect of ALL the drugs she offered. I thought, in that moment, "The disease itself is life-altering and can be fatal, as if that's not enough, but now you want to give me a drug that could be fatal? NO, MA'AM!

She, then, gave me several pamphlets and brochures that reiterated what each drug offered and sent me on my way. I was tasked with the gruesome assignment of deciding my fate. I held my head up, although that's not what I felt like doing, and walked out of the exam room, into the lobby, and down what seemed like a very long hallway to the elevator. Every moment after hearing those letters, MS, was magnified!

How could such a short sentence that contained two letters alter my entire 42 years of existence? "YOU HAVE MS."

We left the doctor's office in silence. I didn't know what to say. My aunt didn't know what to say. We, speechlessly, processed this new reality.

I didn't cry. I couldn't. I found out later that Multiple Sclerosis (MS) can affect your ability to cry. This was just one of the abilities that this thief robbed from me.

My aunt has experienced being in many rooms where my name had been called proclaiming good news. Tralyne Usry, celebrating five years, ten years of training in ballet, tap, and jazz! Tralyne Usry, honor roll student. Tralyne Usry, graduate of high school, college, and graduate school. Tralyne Usry, featured in four magazines. Tralyne Usry, writer of stage plays, author of books, preacher, teacher, poet, leader, etc., but this time, the announcement that followed my name did not merit celebration. Tralyne Usry, YOU ARE SICK AND IT'S INCURABLE!

Chapter 3
A Bumpy Road

"Shet up!" my momma yelled while looking at me very sternly. She, then, turned back to her friend who'd come to our house to pick her up. It was Friday night, and they were on their way to party.

My heart sank. I felt smaller than a pregnant ant. I was embarrassed. I was broken. I was so many things that my 16yearold mind couldn't process! The only thing I was sure of was that I wanted out. I no longer wanted to be in my momma's house.

My mom finished getting dressed and she and "Lil Bit" left. I couldn't wait until they pulled out of the driveway. So, as soon as I heard the car doors slam shut, I ran to the phone. "Grandma," I said with tears in my eyes, "Can I come live with you?" "Well, of course you can, but what's wrong," she questioned. "My momma just yelled at me for no reason, telling me to shet up, and I ain't even do nothing!"

She listened and interjected a few 'ums,' 'huhs' and 'ok, babys.' Shortly thereafter, she uttered words that would change my life. "Well, you can come tomorrow after I talk to yo momma. If she says it's ok, you can come stay with me and your granddaddy." Mrs. Ethel Mitchell was the best thing to me since sliced bread. My grandma was my hero, a position she would occupy forever or as long as I wasn't mad at her.

The next day, I awaited my momma's yelling. I just knew she would fuss after talking to my grandma. So, I sat on edge all day. Later that evening, my mom came to my bedroom door with some large black plastic trash bags. I thought I was about to be put on trash duty. "Here. Put your clothes in here, and don't take too long. I'mma drop you off at your grandma's house on my way to bowling.

I jumped up from my bed and speedily threw everything I could into those trash bags. I couldn't believe she was actually letting me go!

The ride to my granny's house was somber. Frankie Beverly and Maze wailed through the speakers as they often do, while my mom drove the car as if she was alone. Conversation wasn't a focus. She seemed to always be focused on an end goal, accomplishing whatever she set out to do.

The ride seemed like forever as I grappled with the rollercoaster of my emotions and thoughts. "Is my Momma mad at me? Is she ever gonna speak to me again? What did my grandma say to her? Am I a bad daughter? Have I betrayed my momma?"

We pulled into the driveway. My mom put the car in park and took the key out of the ignition. "Get all your stuff out the trunk, cause I ain't coming back," she said, in between puffs of her cigarette. As she exhaled, and her breath and smoke filled the car, I knew for sure that she was mad at me. She was a firebreathing dragon, unleashing her wrath on the object of her disdain. It was a good thing that real fire didn't come from that cigarette. Otherwise, I would've been barbecue.

She went inside and didn't look back.

I walked into the house, dragging all I could carry down the hall, to the room where I'd slept many times before, but this time was different. I wasn't going back home. This was my new home.

After three trips back to the car, I finished. All my worldly possessions filled seven huge black trash bags.

"You done," she questioned. "Yes, ma'am," I replied. Her voice faded. The front door closed with force.

Yep, she's mad! She didn't even say 'bye.' The tears quickly ran down my face as I sat down on the bed, "What did I do? Why is she so angry with me? She yelled at me. I didn't yell at her."

My grandma now had to drive me to school because I was now living way out of district. High school was tough enough. Adding this wrinkle to her day was not helpful at all but I made it.

Granny and I fussed every day! The sweet lady that I once knew disappeared the day I moved in with her and my grandpa!

She would ask me a million questions that I didn't want to answer. "Who you talking to on the phone? Who's that girl you was talking to after school? What time did you go to bed last night?" When? What? Where? Who? How? The questions were endless!

All of this frustration uncovered my battle with depression.

I walked out of my Granny's house one day, wearing a long purple trench coat. But before I left, I wrote a note: "I'm tired and I can't do this anymore. I love you all. Goodbye!"

My destination was clear in my mind as I cried and walked my way to Sandbar Ferry Road. Eighteen-wheelers and semitrucks traveled this road frequently. My intention was clear, too. I was going to stand in front of one of those 18wheelers and end my life.

It seemed like it took forever for me to reach my destination. It was only about five minutes. Just before I was about to walk into the road, my heart was tugged. I had not told my best friend "goodbye."

There was a payphone on the side of the corner store. I walked to that phone to make what I thought was my last phone call.

"Hey, Mookie," she said. "How are you?" "I'm tired and I just don't want to be here anymore. I just called to tell you 'goodbye' and 'I love you.'"

"Wait, where are you?" she questioned. "I'm on Sandbar Ferry Road at the payphone but I won't be here long. I just want you to know, I love you." Tears flooded my eyes and my voice.

"I'm coming," she said. "Will you please wait for me? Stay right there. Don't move, please."

I could now hear tears in her voice, too.

"Okay", I said.

"Mookie, promise me that you'll wait right there for me."

"I promise," I said. Just as I hung the phone up, two 18wheelers came barreling down Sandbar Ferry Road at top speed. The reality of what I'd planned to do hit me like a ton of bricks and my crying turned into wailing! I leaned against the wall of the store and sank to the ground.

My life was changing once again.

Chapter 4
She's A Young One

I was a member of a historical church in Augusta, Georgia. I started there in my momma's womb. I was dedicated there as a baby, baptized there as a child, and disappointed there as a teenager. It was there that I learned that "everything that glitters ain't gold."

This place was where I learned that people who sing and say the Lord's name can use those same lips to cuss, shout, and condemn the very brother or sister that they smiled and grinned with on prior occasions.

The tall, frail, elderly pastor could never say my name right and my family thought that was just hilarious. "Hey, Latreen!" he'd say, every time.

He passed away and everything at the church changed. My world seemed to be changing all the time.

The search for a new pastor began. We had a visiting minister almost every week and then a church meeting, periodically, after that to decide if we, the congregation, liked the preacher and wanted him to become our new pastor. This is when hidden animosities were uncovered and anger spewed like venom from a snake's mouth. "Sit down and shet up. We don't want him here," the deacon yelled. "He doesn't have enough education!" "Yeah," said a few members of the congregation. "Who do you think you are? This ain't your church," said a lady in a pink dress.

I watched in amazement! The familiar scent of freshly permed hair, floral perfume, and Sunday dinner cooking turned into sour words, and malodorous body language. This was no longer the place of safety that I grew up with all my life. I, for the first time in my life, was scared to be in church.

My mom must've seen the fear in my eyes, so she motioned for me to stand and come out of the pew because we were leaving. We weren't at the end of the pew, so we had to move around a few legs to get to the end of the row. "Oww!" yelled a lady whose toe I accidentally stepped on while trying to pass. She was a girthy lady. So, getting around her was no small task. "Excuse me! I apologize," I said quickly. "You're not excused, and you just need to sit yo ass down!" she exclaimed.

There, in that moment, even more of what I knew to be church was shattered. "She said a cuss word in church," I thought my eyes must've revealed my thought. "What you looking at me like that for? Yeah, I said it!"

My thought quickly shifted to concern. "Does she know who my momma is and that she hears everything she's saying," I questioned, in my mind of course. I dare not utter those words.

"Wait a minute! Who you talkin' to? That's my child and you don't talk to her like that," my mom said.

The meeting's attention now shifted to us. "Eewwh," said a kid on the back row. "They 'bout ta fight," said his friend standing next to him. They had no idea how much of a possibility that was.

One of the trustees came running over. "Ladies, ladies. Must I remind you that you are in church," he said.

"I don't give a damn where we are! She better get her daughter and teach her some respect!" the lady yelled.

We had made it out of the pew. Standing in the aisle, the lady called my mom a female dog. "Oh, no, you didn't. Nobody calls me that!" my mom yelled and in a split second, my momma lunged forward to grab the lady, but the trustee jumped between them.

"Momma, let's go," I said as tears streamed down my cheeks. What is happening?

The trustee ushered us down the aisle holding my mom around the waist. She was still trying to tear herself loose and get back to the lady when we were out of the front door. "Just calm down, Karen. Come back whenever you're ready to be calm," said the trustee.

I knew that wouldn't be that night. My mom was livid!

All of this sparked my search. I wanted to know the truth about Jesus! "This can't be it," I thought. "This can't be what life with Jesus is supposed to be like!"

There were a few more of these church meetings before a pastor was chosen. I thought the madness would stop. It did not. It got worse.

The church voted and an overwhelming majority chose this one pastor. He came into the church with excitement and zeal. He preached things from the Bible that I had never heard and apparently some of the powers that be had never heard. While these things excited me, the "big wigs" were quite unhappy.

My grandfather was a deacon, and very devoted. So, he was present during the meetings of dissention. I heard him and my grandma talking in their bedroom one night. "They talking about getting rid of him," my granddaddy said. "But why," asked my grandma. "They said they don't like how he preach, and what he preach and the way he wants to change the structure of the church. He say deacons ain't supposed to make all the decisions, but the pastor supposed to make the decisions based on what he hear from God."

"Well, what's wrong with that," Grandma asked. I could hear the concern in her voice.

I tiptoed back to my room hoping they didn't hear me.

There was more talk. "They did what?" my grandma yelled into the receiver of the phone. "Arrested him? For what? Well, he's supposed to go to the church. He da pastor. Restraining order? What in the world?"

That was Sunday. My granny was on the phone every day that week with a new update that meant more and more drama for the pastor and everyone that supported him.

My world was changing yet again.

"We're going to church," Grandma said. I looked around the room trying to understand why that announcement was necessary. We went to church every Sunday. I was confused.

The drive to church was quiet. My granddaddy wasn't talking. Not unusual. My grandmama wasn't talking. This had never occurred in my entire life. I became nervous.

We pulled into the parking lot. There was a gaggle of people standing together in a huddle. "What's happening?" I asked. My granddaddy didn't know. My grandmama didn't know. Confusion filled the car.

We got out of the car apprehensively.

"They done locked the church. Chained the doors, so we can't get in," said a very angry supporter of the pastor. "I can't believe them," chimed the lady in a purple dress.

The pastor walked into the crowd shortly thereafter. "We must be calm," Pastor said. " We're going to remain Godly despite the opposition," Pastor said. "We're gonna knock on the door and ask them can we come in and pray."

The crowd agreed and walked to the front of the church, up a long flight of green carpet covered steps and the pastor knocked on the front door. There was no answer. He knocked again and again and again. No answer. One of the deacons who was a supporter emerged in the front of the crowd. "Snap!" A loud sound rang out and the crowd started moving forward through the doors. As I entered the doors, I looked on the ground. There in a pile of rubble were the chains that once held the doors of the church closed. The deacon stood by, box cutters in hand, ushering the supporters into the church.

"We shall overcome. We shall overcome," sang the very loud deacon, affixed in a chair at the front of the church. "We shall overcome someday-ay-ay-ay-ay," he continued. "Is this what the civil rights movement felt like?" I questioned.

We walked down the aisle and sat down in a pew a few rows from the front. The deacon continued to sing while my pastor walked into the pulpit.

"Leave! We don't want you here," yelled a parishioner from the back of the church.

The pastor rested his hands on the rostrum. "We just want to pray and then we'll leave," the pastor reassured the angry mob.

The singing deacon left his chair at the front of the church, but he didn't go far. He sat quietly on the front pew.

The pastor prayed and quietly began to leave the pulpit when the singing deacon rose from the front pew.

"Well, if he can pray, we can pray, too," he chanted. He reached for the mic that was positioned near a podium on the side of the pulpit.

"Boom!" The deacon hit the ground. He fainted right before our eyes.

"I can pray! I can pray," said his wife as she stood up from the front pew. She stepped over her husband's body, grabbed the mic, and began to pray.

What was happening? Why was this happening? Where was God? This is not what these same people taught me all my life about God.

I wiped the profusely flowing tears from my cheeks when all of a sudden, I felt something in my belly. I grabbed my stomach and began to cry harder. My momma heard me and walked to the pew where I was sitting to get me. She ushered me out of the seat, down the aisle, and out the front door.

I walked to the car knowing that there had to be something better than what I was experiencing. The picture of God presented to me from childhood was not being reflected by these adult role models. Was this God real or had I been deceived all 18 years of my life? I felt lied to.

As a result, my quest began. I had to find Jesus for myself. I started visiting other churches, ones that emphasized teaching the Bible. It was then that I was introduced to the concept of salvation. This was a foreign concept. All I ever knew about entrance into Heaven and God being pleased with me hinged on church membership and paying church dues. There was never a mention of salvation.

"You must be born again," said the pastor standing behind the rostrum in the front of the church. I'd never seen a preacher come out of the pulpit to preach. Teaching Bible study, AND standing close to the congregation? I sat in amazement.

"Romans 10:9-10 makes the plan of salvation clear. You must believe in your heart AND confess with your mouth, then you are saved. You are born again," he said. "Yeah, Pastor," said one of the congregants.

"Wait! She's talking out loud to the pastor, and it's not because she disagrees with him, but because she was encouraging him to continue speaking?" My thoughts were all over the place along with my emotions. I was happy. I was confused. I was sad. I was intrigued. I felt so many things, but what I didn't feel was unsafe. This felt like what I knew church to be but even better. This felt like home.

I accepted Jesus Christ as my Lord and Savior!

I visited that church for a few more weeks and learned more about the Bible. It seemed like I learned more in a few short weeks than I'd learned in my 18 years of being raised in a Baptist church.

One night after Bible study, I gathered my things to leave when I was approached by one of the ladies of the church. I'd seen her every time I came to church and she was very friendly. I thought she was just coming to give me a hug and thank me for coming. This was customary.

"What's your name?" she asked. "Tralyne," I replied. "Oh! That's a pretty name." "Thank you," I replied.

"Listen! There's a service across town tomorrow night with this well-known prophetess. I think you'd really enjoy it. You wanna meet me there?" she questioned. "Sure, just tell me where it is, and the time, and I'll be there," I said excitedly.

She was right! There were people dancing, shouting, singing, crying, and yelling out praises to God. There was no one bickering or fighting. Everyone appeared to get along. This felt like how church should be.

The prophetess preached, and preached, and preached. I felt amazing. I was overjoyed and overwhelmed by the presence that I felt. It was familiar. I'd felt the same presence in the church I visited but never in my Baptist church. I never wanted to leave.

"Listen! I hear the Lord saying that we need to shut-in and pray," the prophetess announced. "I want you to meet me back here at 1:00 am. Don't be late because the doors will be locked.

Meet me back here and let's pray. The Lord is going to meet us here," she said.

There was an immediate angst. I wanted to come back to service but I knew my grandma was going to protest.

"One o'clock in the morning? One o'clock in the mornin'? Who goes to church at 1 o'clock in the morning?" she questioned. And you've already been there for four hours. She didn't pray in those four hours?" My Granny was livid at the thought. "Grandma, I'm going to church. It's my best friend's church. The doors will be locked. So, I'll be safe. Please!"

After about an hour and a half of rationalizing, coercing, and outright begging, she finally gave me permission to go, reluctantly.

"You be careful, and call me when you get there, in the parking lot, and then again when you get inside the church," she said. "Yes, ma'am," I said as I hurried out the door. I couldn't be late. I'd be locked out.

I made it with only a few minutes to spare. I complied with all of my grandma's demands and excitedly went to find my seat. "12:59" was displayed on my watch.

An aroma filled the room. The smell was "woodsy" like oak or cedarwood. Women were crying and praying. Some were walking back and forth, crying, chanting, and speaking in an unknown language. I'd heard something like that in the church I'd been visiting but I had no idea what it was.

The prophetess came to the pulpit and began to speak in that strange language. She, then, encouraged the audience to speak in their "heavenly prayer language." "Who wants it but doesn't have a heavenly prayer language?" she inquired.

It was as if she heard my thoughts.

"Come down to the altar." I couldn't get down there fast enough.

Women were standing in front of the pulpit at the altar. Their lips were moving but I couldn't hear what they were saying. As I got closer, I heard the unknown language again. I wasn't clear about what was happening, but I knew I was supposed to go to one of those ladies.

"Hey, Baby! You want to receive the Holy Ghost with the evidence of speaking in tongues?" she asked. "Is that what ya call it? Is that what it is?" I thought. "Yes, ma'am," I said. "Have you accepted Jesus as your personal Lord and Savior," she asked. "No, ma'am," I replied. "Well, first things first. Do you believe that Jesus died for yours sins?" she asked. "Yes!" Do you believe He rose again? Do you accept Him in your heart as your Lord and Savior?" "Yes, ma'am," "You are now saved! Welcome to the family." She hugged me really tight and seemed like she'd never let me go, and I didn't want her to. I felt brand new! March 3, 1995 at 2:30 am, my life changed yet again!

She released me and told me to call the name of Jesus over and over again. So, I did. Then, I was embraced again.

"Say His name. Say the name of Jesus," the unknown woman holding me from behind chanted repeatedly in my ear. The warm tears stained my cheeks.

All around me were like-positioned women, young and old, crowded the altar, intensely calling the name of Jesus.

I felt a familiar ebbing in my belly. It was the same feeling I felt when I began to cry out in my Baptist church. I would learn later that this was the spirit of intercession. I buckled over. A warm sensation covered my body and peace filled my soul. I received the gift, the Holy Ghost!

Chapter 5
A Whole New World

I became very committed to the church. I was there for every service.

I was introduced to a pastor during a night of Bible study at my regular church, Pastor Aline P. Scott. Her knowledge of the Word, the revelation, and the delivery of the Word of God drew me immediately.

I sought out her church and joined the ministry shortly thereafter. I became a member, remained faithful to studying the Word, and learning more about God and eventually yielded to the ebbing with which I had grown familiar, the unction of the Holy Ghost. I was licensed to be a minister there at the tender age of 18 to preach the gospel.

I had a zeal, thirst, and hunger for the Lord that was insatiable. It governed my every move. I belonged to the Lord!

Chapter 6

Caregiver (Part 1)

I started working at the DFACS (Department of Family and Children Services) shortly after I graduated from college. My caseload was over 500 and it was populated with multiple generations of families.

I enjoyed helping others.

One day, my friend, a couple of cubicles away, called me while I was sitting at my desk. "Hey girl, you busy?" she asked. "Always, but what's up? You need something?" I asked. "I have someone here who wants to meet you." "Ok, I'll be there in a second." I backed away from my desk and walked to her cubicle.

"Hey," said the unidentified woman sitting across from my friend. "Hi," I replied. "Yo daddy named Tom?" she asked. "No," I responded. She continued. "Yes, it is. His real name 'Tommy' but he calls "hisself" Jimmy." At this point, I got nervous. I wasn't afraid of the woman. I just started to think, "Is this another woman saying she has a child by my father? Do I have yet another sibling?" This was not an abnormal occurrence. My daddy liked the ladies.

I said, "Ok." She looked at my friend, her caseworker, and said, "Yeah, that's him," as she sat back in her chair, folded her arms and rolled her eyes.

I told her to have a good day and walked back to my cubicle. I heard no more about this woman until two weeks later.

My supervisor called me while I was sitting at my desk and asked me to come to her office. Once I got to her door, she invited me to come in and have a seat. She asked me about the woman I'd met two weeks prior and inquired about our interaction that day in my friend's cubicle. I told her what had happened, and she explained that the woman was accusing me of divulging information about her case. I explained that I'd talked to no one about the woman and that she was not telling the truth. My supervisor said okay and told me to go back to my desk.

I did and a few minutes later, someone came and told me that I was wanted upstairs to meet with the director of the department.

I went to a conference room, filled with an oversized table, and chairs, and I sat down and waited for the director.

She came in, greeted me, and sat on the other end of the table, as far from me as possible. That was a sign. This outcome will not be good.

"Ms. Usry, we're gonna have to let you go. It is company policy that we keep our client's personal information confidential and you did not," she said.

My eyes stretched, my jaw dropped, and my heart raced. "I've just been fired behind a lie, and no one is believing me. Had they asked my friend? She was there. Did she lie on me, too? What just happened?"

I left the conference room disappointed to say the least. I went home. My Granny asked as I walked through the door, "Why you home so early?" "I got fired Grandma," I replied. "Fired? Fired? Why?" I explained what happened. She was disappointed and upset that I'd been mistreated, and falsely accused.

"You can get another job," she said after some time of fussing. I responded, "I could, but you need help with Granddaddy. So, I'll just stay here and help you until the Veteran's Administration (VA) gets you more help."

My grandfather, Joseph Mitchell, was a retired army veteran. He'd had strokes and become partially paralyzed.

The stroke also affected his throat, so he stopped talking, and eating most things.

My Granny was his caregiver. I'd help occasionally, when she'd allow me to help, but she was the primary. She'd lift him, bathe him, feed him, take him in and out of the bed, dress him, and everything. She eventually tore the rotator cuff in her right shoulder cup but that didn't stop her. She was determined.

The VA eventually approved benefits for my Grandpa, and even approved them retroactively so my Granny was able to have the house remodeled to make it handicap accessible. She was also able to hire caregivers to assist with my granddaddy's care.

I'd been praying all along for this VA approval, and direction for my next move. I wanted to attend grad school but not unless my grandparents were taken care of properly.

During this time, unfortunately, my father was shot in the neck at his place of business. After leaving the hospital, he required care, as well.

My interactions with my father before this point were few and far in between. I went to his shop only to ask for money, but this changed one day, prior to him being shot.

I walked into the place formerly known as "The Windjammer," my father's nightclub, now my father's trucking business, "Simpson's Trucking," after my grandaunt's last name. I was, hastily, greeted by my father. "What you want, Tralyne? I'm busy and I ain't got no money," he yelled.

With tears in my eyes, pain in my heart, and trembling in my voice, I said, "I don't want another dime from you! I just want you to be my father. He stopped in his tracks, midstride trying to walk away from me, and was frozen for a few seconds before he walked over to where I was and hugged me. Before that moment, I couldn't remember a time where he'd hugged me . It didn't feel odd though. It felt as if it somehow replaced all of the missed hugs from before.

He held my hand and escorted me to a table, pulled out my chair and asked me to sit down. He explained how he'd always been so busy, and he didn't really know how to be a father. With tears in his eyes, while holding my hand, he said, "I'm sorry, I'll try to do better."

All of the years before vanished with that one sentence! I finally have a daddy!

We spent time together often after that. So, when he was shot, it was only natural that I became his caregiver.

I guess caring for my grandfather helped to prepare me for taking care of my father.

I'd do it all over again! Those two men both impacted my life in different ways but still impactful.

Mentoring Moment (E. Evaluate)

Evaluate means to judge or determine the significance, worth, or quality of, assess. This phase, once completed, will cause you to assess your challenges as they are and to see all parts. This will prepare you to properly dismantle them in the next phase.

In any of the aforementioned times in my life, I had to evaluate, determine the worth or quality of something and make decisions accordingly. Was my commitment to the church producing anything beneficial? What's the significance of the diagnosis of MS? I had to evaluate each situation separately to prepare to dismantle when and where needed.

Turn to page 5 in your H.O.W. Workbook and begin Phase 1, Evaluate.

Chapter 7

Going Off to Grad School

I always loved movies. I was fascinated by that form of storytelling. I also knew that filmmakers made lots of money and I was determined not to be broke.

I was also overly committed to my church and needed a way of escape. So, I applied to graduate school at Regent University in Virginia Beach, Virginia. I was accepted into their Directing for Film & Television Master's Degree program. I was approved for loans, secured housing, and packed up to pursue my dream of becoming a film maker. My grandparents were secure, my daddy was better, and my dreams were waiting.

I grew fond of the school very quickly and was matriculating well up until the last semester before completion of the program. In February 2004, my grandfather died. In March, my best friend, Cheryl, died. And in April, my dad died. I was devastated to say the least. My grades plummeted.

I left grad school grieving the death of my father, my grandfather, my best friend, and my master's degree in film and television.

Chapter 8
She "Spits"

All was not lost during my time in grad school. Dormant gifts were uncovered, poetry writing, and performing poetry.

I was a part of a church that celebrated the arts. The pastor was a playwright and loved all forms of creative artistry. The environment was ripe and conducive for creativity.

I'd always dreamed of writing, and specifically writing poetry once I was introduced to the works of Dr. Maya Angelou but I never thought I would write as well as she, so I didn't try.

The environment in that little church in Virginia changed all of that. I started to believe that I could.

I was also employed with a major Christian ministry as a prayer counselor. One of the requirements of every employee was that we attend two corporate worship assemblies each year: New Year's Eve and Founders Day.

On New Year's Day, 2002, I found myself in the presence of believers from all nationalities and faith levels, worshipping the Lord. The presence of God was so tangible and could be felt by anyone with a pulse. The praise and worship team sang like angels. The musicians played like they created the instruments themselves. The atmosphere was so perfect. My heart was free. My head was lifted. My countenance was bright, and my soul was in love all over again. I wrote, "Have You Ever?"

Have You Ever?

Have you ever?

Have you ever had anybody to blow your mind

With like just one line?   Say
something so sweet
 That makes you feel complete

Have you ever had a brother say something so fierce That
through all your defenses pierce?
You know the lines that some men spout
Momentarily eliminating and relieving any doubt
You know lines like
For you, I'll cross an ocean
Without a notion
Or with you my sweet
I'm complete
You my universe
My stars
My world You my
girl!
Have you ever had a lover A lover
like no other?
So passionate So sweet Have you mesmerized for a week?
Have you ever known bliss From one
single solitary kiss Have you ever?
Well, I never
Not until I met a lover so real   So deep
so steep
His words so sweet
One line, I forgive
Translation, you may live
Eternity is my hook
 The kiss of forever
It is written in the book
He paralyzes my senses
I need no defenses
I can't taste, touch smell, or see
The width of His adoration for me
He permeates my existence

Made me a witness
A partaker of His glory
Yeah, this is my story
For me, He crossed eternity
The depth of sin was not too great
For you my love, I will wait
Wait on the cross until the work is done
Until with me, you'll be secured by the son
And when it was finished
Full fellowship replenished
I cannot be without you
I will not allow
Anything to separate
This is my solemn vow
Have you ever known a love like this?

I was tasked by my pastor, shortly thereafter to share a poem for Valentine's Day. I was both excited and nervous. I prayed through my anxiety and I decided to share "Have You Ever?" which was later published in my first poetry book, "Aesthetically, Audibly Me."

The performance was celebrated with thunderous applause and a standing ovation! This was the first of many. I became an award-winning, televised spoken word artist! She "spits" and
"the rest is history!"

Chapter 9
Teacher, Teacher

My world had changed once again. I moved to Richmond, Virginia and became a member of Greater Touch of Compassion Ministries under the leadership of Apostle Ezreaonne Jackson. I grew so much while I was there.

I was ordained as an elder.

I learned a lot ... what to do and what not to do.

An incident occurred that drove me into a depression. I was back living with my aunt. So, I went into the basement and stayed there. I no longer felt welcomed in the church, but I loved the people there. So, I had to pray about my return to the church. I wanted to leave but a very large part of me wanted to stay.

I'd been evicted from my apartment in Glenn Allen and I had no job because the two businesses where I worked had closed.

During the eviction, members of my aunt's church came to the rescue; Alton and Cynthia Mosely. Alton helped me to pack up the apartment. He rented a U-Haul. He hired two men and they loaded the U-Haul. Alton drove me to my aunt's and unloaded all of my earthly possessions! I would not have made it through without him and his wife!

I went back to the church after I felt what was the leading of the Lord. My church eventually dissolved. My pastor moved back to California. I subsequently moved to North Carolina, all in a matter of months but it felt like days. It was all happening too fast. Everything I knew to be solid and sure was now water on a sidewalk in the heat, quickly evaporated.

I became a Teacher's Assistant in an Exceptional Children's (EC) classroom. It was comprised of five students, each with their own unique special needs. I was in heaven!

Each student presented a puzzle that I considered my personal duty to figure out and that I did with the help of the other teacher's assistant, Wanda Motley, who was far more efficient than me.

We worked tirelessly every day, addressing the students' needs academically, emotionally, socially, whatever the day presented, because each day was unique.

"You plan Social Studies and I'll plan Science," I said to the other teacher's assistant. "You know I already got it, right?" she said smiling. "Of course, you do. I don't know I even said anything," I said smiling.

In my head, I thought, "I hope this lead teacher actually does some planning and teaching this week." This was a regular challenge each week. We, assistants, found ourselves planning ALL of the lessons because when the lead teacher did anything, it was a video on YouTube or a worksheet that came nowhere close to addressing the needs of the students.

Observations were a normal occurrence. The administrative staff would "pop-up" to see what was happening in the class.

"Make it make sense," I chimed as I taught reading strategies. The other assistant was sitting with one of our students who had a tendency to try to run out of the classroom. The lead teacher was sitting at her desk doing something on her computer. The principal, the assistant principal, and the interning principal walked through the classroom door. I could hear the whistle you hear in those old Westerns when a gun fight was about to take place. The lead teacher was not in place.
She was not doing her job.

She looked up, quickly closed her computer, and said, "Thank you, Ms. Usry."

She quickly moved to take over the class. She fumbled to find something to do. "What sound does "D" make?" she asked. "Duh!" the students yelled with confusion on their faces. "Why is she asking us the sound of a letter? We are not in kindergarten. We are in the 3rd, 4th, and 5th grade," imagined their thoughts.

The administrators, sitting at a table in the back of the classroom, watched as the lead teacher had no idea what she was doing. After about 30 minutes, they left. Soon after, the lead teacher sat back down behind her desk, and the other teacher's assistant began to lead the class. Back to our norm.

These pop-up visits by administration happened more frequently, and the lead teacher noticed this pattern, so she started being in front of the class more often. She showed the students video after video, after video and she gave them a ton of worksheets. The students were lost. This confusion sparked unwanted behaviors and disruptions. Something had to be done.

Ms. Motley and I became more aggressive in our teaching. The lead teacher would present a video or worksheet, after which, we'd break the students into groups, take the concepts presented and create more palatable lessons geared towards each student's ILP (individual learning plan).

This effort did not go unnoticed. "Ms. Usry, can I speak with you for a moment?" the interning principal questioned.

"Sure," I said as I followed her into the hallway. "Why aren't you a teacher? You have the skills and you're doing it in here every day. What's the holdup? Why haven't you gotten your license?" she inquired.

"I didn't get my undergrad degree in Education and I can't afford to go back to school," I said.

"You don't need to go back to school. You just need to take the Praxis."

"I didn't know that, but I can't afford that. That test is expensive, and I don't have that money right now," I insisted.

"Is that the only hold-up? Is that what's stopping you? Come by my office sometime today and we will register you for the test."

"Wait! WHAT?" I don't have the money for the test, and I can't ask you to...," she interrupted me.

"You didn't ask! I'm volunteering. So, I'll see you later today when you come by my office to register for this test," she said and walked away from me back down the hall. I didn't get to protest, question, or even refuse.

My life was about to change, yet again.

I prepared for the test for a few months because the test wasn't scheduled until June. The wait for the test results was torture.

The next school year started, and I was transferred to another classroom. The lead teacher in my old classroom was disgruntled with me. We no longer got along.

My principal asked if I had received the results of the test almost every day. "No," I'd say with a frown.

I got the results one day while in the classroom just before I had to escort one of the students to another class. I saw my principal when I got halfway down the hall.

I greeted him with the world's biggest grin. "You got the results?" he questioned, grinning from ear to ear. I shook my head in the affirmative. I passed the test!

Change. A week or two later, I was moved into my own classroom, and I began teaching Kindergarten!

Chapter 10

My Heartbeat

This time was hilarious to say the least! My Granny REQUIRED nightly phone calls, not because she needed anything other than to know my every activity of every day. These conversations were so funny that I had to post some of them on Facebook!

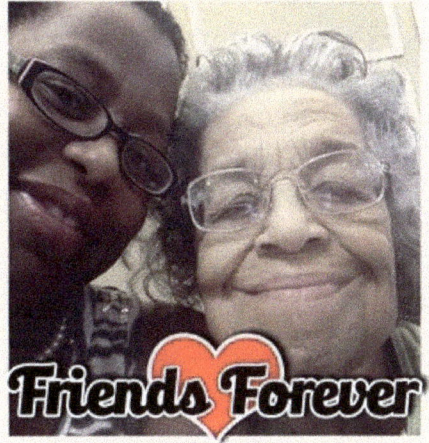

On September 27, 2014, I wrote:

Granny just said, and I quote, "Get some rest so you can be hot and poppin' in the morning." GOODNIGHT, SAINTS! I can't take anymore!!! lol! This lady NEVER ceases to amaze me!!!

June 25, 2014

"So, I called my Granny to tell her that I was going to bed early because I have an early day tomorrow. First of all, she set a world record; she only told me 'bye' three times, and only started two NEW stories! Lol! Second of all, she told me to go to sleep, and think about her singing; "RockEEbye, baby, on the treetop. When the wind blows, the cradle will rock. When the bow breaks, SOMETHING, SOMETHING or another will fall. And down will come baby, cradle and all." Betcha didn't know the remix!! RockEE bye, baby, and something, something or another.... I LOVE MY GRANNY!!"

April 17, 2014

"Granny and that hat yesterday..."

Granny: *"I meant to tell you to take your hat back with you and I'd wear it when you come home."*

Me: *"You did tell me, but I told you that you could keep the hat because I don't wear it."*

Granny: *"Well, I thought you might wanna start wearing it since you seen how good it looked on me." She's so modest! Lol!"*

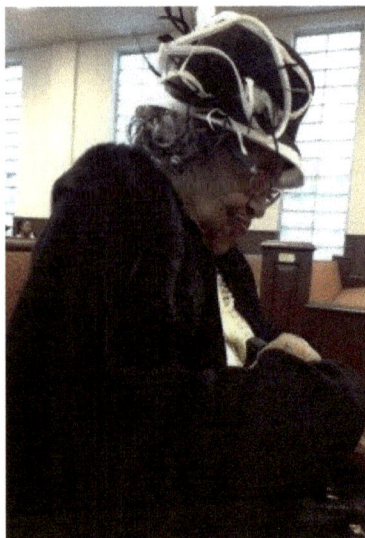

April 5, 2015

So, y momma was talking   to   Granny   this morning....

Momma: *Where you going this morning?*

Granny: *I don't know.*

Momma: *Last night, you told me you was going to meet a boyfriend. What happened?*   **Granny**: *That fell through.*
#ImDoneAGAIN

#MyGranny #MyLegacy #92YearsAndCounting

The comedy was just as hilarious when we were together! I posted some of those times on Facebook, as well!

On December 14, 2012, I wrote:

My Grandma just saw this pic on TV and said, "Oooohhh, Tralyne! You made it on TV!" Really, Grandma?! Lol! Eighty- nine years old and still got jokes!

#CLASSIC!! LOVE HER FOREVER!"

(Christmas movie)

November 27, 2013

"So, I gave my old Nook to my Granny, so she could read, thinking I was doing something!! She was excited and very appreciative as she began reading. Then, I showed her a word search game on the iPad! What did I do that for? She has asked me, more than once, if MY iPad was hers!!!! Lol! Houston, we have a problem!! — feeling blessed."

December 25, 2013

"So, I ran into my Grandma's room jumping up and down like I was five saying, "It's Christmas! It's Christmas! Santa Claus' been here!!" My Granny turns over and says, "You don't ever go to sleep, do you?" BAHHHAAAHAA!!! I am weak! Merry

Christmas!"

December 21, 2013

"I called my Granny when I was not far from the house, because my Aunt said she was waiting up for me to tell her that I had my key. She said, "I'm not waiting up for you (elevated pitch) but I'll be sitting right cheer in this chair TIL you get cheer."

#lovemyGranny   #90yearsandcounting   #StillSprite #Legendary"

There were also moments of great wisdom, determination, and faith!

On September 3, 2010, I wrote:

"My Granny was staring at the wall and I asked her what she was looking at. She said she was enjoying the view. I asked what view? She said just the view from sitting up and feeling better! Day 4 .... She IS ALIVE and shall continue to declare the glorious works of GOD!"

September 6, 2010

"Granny got out of the bed at 8:30 AM, ate breakfast, and decided to cook dinner for tonight. She cut up the collards, sweet potatoes, and sent me to the store for the milk to make cornbread from scratch. She said, as she was going to her room, "I've been thanking the Lord all morning for giving me my feelings back, no pain. I feel like a new person."

Thanks for praying! She is alive ....!

Our relationship was truly epic! I was determined that although she was aging, she'd never feel like a burden, unwanted, or unneeded.

August 31, 2010

I remember, when I was a teenager, scratchin,' greasin,' and rollin' my Grandma's hair was a task I worked HARD to avoid! I hated it! But now, with every part of her hair, every stroke of grease, and every bend of a roller, I thank GOD for these moments! Eighty-seven years and counting! Day 1 of the road to healing! She shall live ....

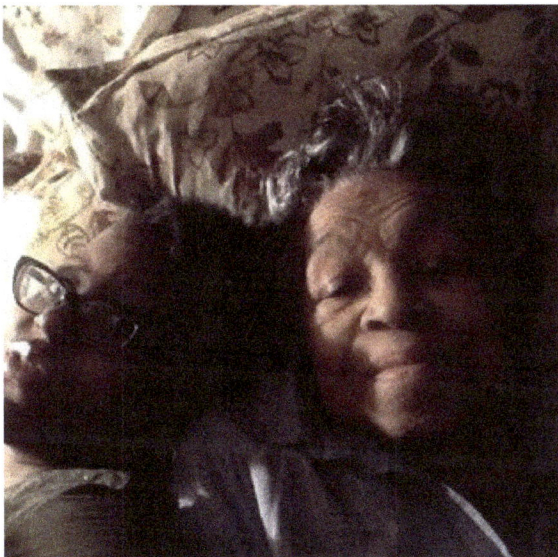

She is my BEST FRIEND FOREVER!

Chapter 11
"An Urban Christmas Carol"

(Photos shown in this chapter were taken by Patrick James of Artistic Design & Photography, unless otherwise noted)

I'd been writing and producing stage plays but on, what I considered to be, a small scale. They were written and produced in different churches and the school where I once worked but I'd never rented a whole theater, held mass calls for actors, hired someone to build a set, or sold event tickets. Whoa!

I, also, wanted to do something that had never been done before.

I created an interactive stage play where the audience, at intermission, voted to decide the direction of the play. The audience decided how the play would end. They followed a link on smart phones given to them at intermission and voted between two endings. The ending with the most votes determined the final acts.

The idea came to me some years back when I was a member of Touch of Compassion Church in Richmond, Virginia. I made fake, hand-held remote controls with two buttons: A or B, and the congregation was asked to pretend that the remotes worked.

The participants made a choice with the press of a button. I had

no idea how to make that remote control a technical reality. I was blessed with someone, years later, who did know how to get the job done; Justin Thomas!   He walked me through all things technical concerning the play. I learned so much from him. He was a very patient teacher and leader.

My aunt was a member of Victory Family Outreach Ministries (VFOM) in Woodbridge, Virginia, and her pastors, Bishop John and Pastor Vivian Reid loved me like I was their own. They graciously opened the doors of their church and allowed me to hold casting calls, auditions, and rehearsals there. *(Facebook Photo)*

Members of the church helped! I don't want to miss any of their names or contributions, so I won't try but know that the church stepped in to help as if I was a member and they each did an amazing job!

The dance team from VFOM, "Oracles of Worship," ministered to the audience, as well!

The "Gospel Warriors,"
a mime team travelled
From Augusta, Georgia
and blessed the crowd!
The process was
arduous, but I learned
so much, what to do
and what not to do!

I had family and friends to attend the
play from far and near ... too many
to name them all. Of course, my AA
 "Always Always"),Crystal, was there!

One group, my sister circle from work, came from North Carolina
to be a part of the crowd, Ebonye, "Toni", and Megan! They took
me out afterwards to celebrate over a meal. They are my sisters for
life.

The play was held at a the A.J. Ferlazzo Building in Woodbridge, Virginia. Ticket sales were phenomenal, and people came from all around the world to witness the world's first and ONLY interactive stage play, "An Urban Christmas Carol!"

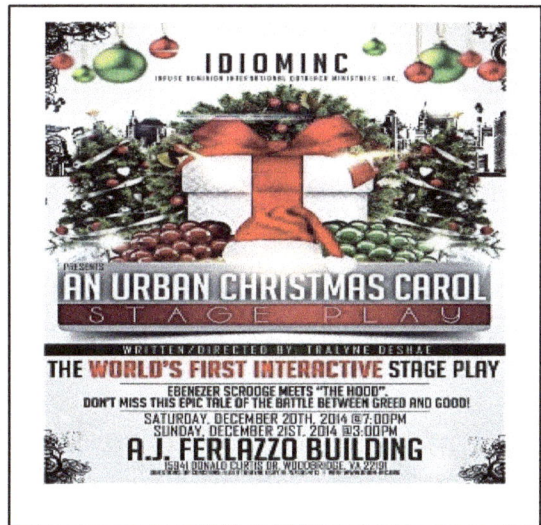

I was a ball of nerves on opening night, so much so that I couldn't keep my thoughts clear. I didn't know whether I was coming or going.

At the intermission, I sat down, took a breath, and asked

Emily, the makeup artist, to beautify me before the show ended.

During this time, Denascia, lead actress, came into the room and saw the angst on my face. She took the control, gave direction to the stage crew, and told me to breathe. We would not have made it without her.

The stage was set for the final acts. I went backstage to listen for the ending.

I asked my brother, Pastor A.J. Mosely, of Divine Unity Christian Church (D.U.C.C.) to lead an altar call before we ended the show inviting people to accept Jesus Christ as their Lord and Savior, if they had not done so previously. He also encouraged and exhorted all of those present.

Once the show was over, the cast was introduced, and the audience applauded.
The emcee was Sharvette Mitchell who is a web designer, radio host, entrepreneur and so much more!

She called my name and I thought I was gonna pass out, but I walked out onto the stage to a standing ovation.

My heart melted!

Included in that overwhelmingly gracious standing audience was my Momma and my Grandma! My life was complete!

Mentoring Moment (D. Dismantle)

Dismantle means to deprive or strip of apparatus, FURNITURE, equipment, defenses, etc. Furniture makes a house livable. I had to begin to strip away the furniture of my challenges; leaving my granny and granddaddy, losing my daddy, becoming discontented with my church. All of these challenges had their own equipment designed to hinder me and prevent forward movement. Let's look at one of these challenges a little closer.

Discontentment with leaving my granddaddy and grandmama: This was designed to keep me from pursuing my dream of going to graduate school for film and television. It was equipped with guilt, worry, and doubt and all of these things rested, made a home (furniture) on lack of finances. All of those misgivings were validated in my thoughts by the fact that I didn't know where the money would come from for my grad school education. I was scared. I had to dismantle that fear. I did so by using the scripture, *"God has not given me the spirit of fear, but of power, and of love, and a sound mind." (2 Timothy 1:7, KJV).* I prayed through it, recited it, and rehearsed in my mind whenever those challenges would present themselves. The more I did so, the less power these challenges held. They were eventually evicted from my house (me)! Dismantled!

Turn to page 16 of your H.O.W. Workbook and begin PHASE 2, Dismantle

Chapter 12
Agape' Village

As a kindergarten teacher, I knew that two things needed to be established; the ability to read, and a love for learning. Without these two attributes, my students would face greater hardships in their academic careers and in life. This knowledge caused me to do lots of research to accomplish these goals. This action was met with many obstacles. I realized, statistically, that students in lowincome areas had very low literacy scores. It was not uncommon to find a 5th grader who couldn't read at all. I knew something had to change.

I was also aware that these same children also lacked access to the performing arts often because their parent or parents lacked the finances to pay for plays, musical instruments or dance lessons.

I felt deep in my heart that this was unfair. These children deserved the same access to the arts as other children. Thus, Agapé Village was born.

I targeted the neighborhood near where I grew up. The housing projects, then called Delta Manor, was filled with children.

I researched the neighboring school's literacy test scores which are a matter of public record. The results did not surprise.

The first year was DEFINITELY a lesson for the teacher. I didn't know anything about running a summer camp. I prayed, researched, and sought wise counsel whenever possible. My Mom's friend, Ms. Mary Fallen, was very familiar with the inner workings of Delta Manor, it's community center, and the neighborhood's children. She'd run an afterschool program and summer camp there for ten years. They knew her well!

She helped me so much with directions on attaining the community center, feeding the students, getting the word out, keeping the students in line, and so much more. I would not have survived the first few years without her.

We partnered with Miracle Making Ministries, a nonprofit organization that focuses on mission's ministry. Through this partnership, we were able to provide bookbags, school supplies, and field trips for the participants, and so much more.

I struggled to find volunteers the first year but that changed as years passed. We began to have varied volunteers: teachers, retired teachers, college students, teenagers, etc. My aunt, sister, god sister, and cousins were recruited to help, as well. We even had a group of volunteers from a large church in Augusta. We were blessed.

A typical day in the life of the camp:

Agapé Village's Daily Schedule

8:30 Breakfast

9:00 Devotional/Prayer

9:30-11:30 Literacy Centers

9:30-9:45 Center 1

9:45-10:00 Center 2

10:00-10:15 Center 3

10:15-10:30 Center 4

10:30-10:45 Break

10:45-11:05

Singing 11:15-11:45

Dancing 11:45-12:15

Acting 12:15-12:30

Break/Prep for lunch 12:30-1:15 Lunch

1:15-1:45 Outdoor play

1:45-2:10 Water/Break/Snack

2:10-3:10 Indoor Games/Crafts

3:10-3:30 Devotional/Treasure box

3:30 Dismissal

The devotion time and literacy centers were my favorites! I taught the kids a Bible story. We'd act it out and the students were, then, responsible for remembering the story until the end of the day. I asked questions, and if the students answered correctly, they were allowed to go into the treasure box and pick a special gift. The goal was to not only teach them about God, but to help them develop a love for the Word and associate reward with knowing the Word of God.

During the literacy centers, the students were divided into age groups and grade levels, challenged and assisted with reading, and reminded of various literacy skills. The goal was to prevent "summer slide." This is the idea that students often lose some of their literacy skills during the summer vacation months causing them to "slide" down on the scale of literary competency.

The students had rest breaks throughout the day. These breaks consisted of trips to the bathroom and water fountain, eating lunch and snacks, and playing outdoors. Our day was full, to say the least.

During the singing, dancing, and acting times, the students were taught some of the fundamentals of each art and they learned things that contributed to the performance at the end of the camp. The students sang, danced, and acted, usually from a play that I wrote.

We invited their parents, as well as the community, to partake of the performance.

We all learned so much. We truly became a village of love (Agapé)!

Chapter 13

A New Church

I lived in Greensboro when I first moved to North Carolina. So, I was commuting two hours a day to Durham for work. I was not a fan of driving, but I had not secured a place in Durham, so commuting was necessary. I was fortunate to live, temporarily, with one of the people responsible for my upbringing, my childhood neighbor, Guila Cooper. When I told her of my job opportunity in North Carolina, she readily offered me a place to stay, "Poo Poo, you can stay with me," she very excitedly exclaimed.

I moved to Greensboro and searched for a church. I needed a place where I could grow, heal, and rest. I'd worked so hard in ministry from 18-years-old. I'd been abused, misused, overlooked and overworked all at the hands of the church. I needed a break.

I found a church that was vibrant, exciting, and SAFE! I enjoyed "the Word" during every Bible study and Sunday service that I attended so much so that even after I found a place to live closer to my job, I still commuted twice a week to attend church. I loved the church so much that the two-hour commute didn't bother me. "A church that is alive is worth the drive."

Chapter 14

Caregiver (Part 2)

"Tralyne, I'm calling because your Grandma hasn't gotten out of bed all day. She's been going to the bathroom, but she just gets back in bed. I was gon' call your aunt to come and take her to the doctor, but I'm not sure if I should just … ," I interrupted, "Call an ambulance! You don't have to wait! Call an ambulance!"

I hung up the phone and began to pack a bag for travel! My heart raced with panic. This behavior was so unlike my Grandma. She was usually awake most of the night, and up first thing in the morning. She'd make her single cup of coffee, since she had the Keurig, and breakfast, and sit at the kitchen table reading the newspaper. "What is wrong with my Granny?" I questioned as I prepared to leave for my trip to Augusta. I'd taken this trip many times before, but this definitely felt different. I began, for the first time, to entertain thoughts of losing my grandma.

That was the longest five-hour drive of my life! I arrived and went directly to my Granny's house. She'd been in the ER for most of the day. The doctors were able to stabilize her and devise a plan for continued care.

I had a million questions. "What happened? What can be done about preventing this from happening again? What was the cause? Is my Granny going to survive?"

I watched her like a hawk that night, walking in and out of her bedroom, praying with every step.

The next morning, she awakened with more energy and I could see the color returning to her face. I was encouraged.

"What you want for breakfast Granny?" I asked. "You already know what I want," she said with a smirk.

Oh, yeah! She was definitely feeling better!

The next few days were consumed with doctor's appointments, prayer, research, prayer, meal prep, prayer, and sleepless nights, and did I mention, PRAYER? I was determined for my Granny to continue to approve and to get better and that she did!

I stayed over the weekend but prepared to go back to North Carolina on Sunday. Granny was up again, making demands, talking on the phone, cooking and doing laundry. I thought, "She's ba-a-a-acck!"

I was in the room repacking my bag when Granny came to the door. "Where you going?" she questioned. "I gotta go to work tomorrow. So, I'm going back to North Carolina," I answered. "You didn't ask me could you go," she retorted. "I'm sorry. What was I thinking? Grandma, can I go back to North Carolina?"

"Nope," she said. "Nope," I questioned. She shook her head. "I want you to stay here with me. You got a warm place to lay your head. I'll feed ya, too. You don't need to go back. You can't go back."

"So, I can't go back to North Carolina, where I work, where I signed a contract, where I pay rent, and where all my belongings are?"

"Well, since you put it like that, I guess I'll let you go, THIS TIME! Next time, I won't be so nice." We both chuckled as she left the door. She was the funniest 90-year-old!

She was doing well for a little while before her health began to decline again slowly. We began to discuss having a caregiver come in more often because my mom was still working, and she needed help. We were able to secure assistance, very able assistance which gave me some comfort but not complete comfort. A year went by and my Granny's health continued to decline.

She stopped walking and going to the bathroom independently.

I started traveling home every weekend to assist with caring for her.

This commute from North Carolina every weekend lasted for about a year and a half. I decided to spend the next summer with her.

During my time of research, I learned about some proven usages of natural foods and their benefits, so I started experimenting. I knew I had to be careful because my Granny's taste buds were very particular.

We had a smoothie in the morning, instead of coffee, a meatless lunch, and a veggie-filled dinner, with a baked meat of some sort and a starch. Fruit was always the snack. No fried foods. No sodas. No Cheetos (one of my Granny's favorites).

I also worked towards changing her atmosphere. I played gospel music while she slept. I prayed with her in the morning and whenever she'd experience a pain. We had Holy Communion once daily and we ventured out to take a ride or go to some place other than the doctor.

One day, we went to the mall. While pushing her in the wheelchair, we walked pass a jewelry store. "Let's go in there," she said pointing back to the jewelry store. This was a good sign! We turned around and she looked at every case, commenting on particular pieces. I asked if she wanted to buy anything after our perusing for about 30 minutes. "Maybe later," she said. My thought was "Later?" I questioned. So, we coming back?

I laughed on the inside as we walked and went back upstairs.

We then saw a massage chair. "You want a massage?" I asked. "How does that work? What I gotta do?" she questioned. "Nothing Grandma, you just gotta sit in this chair."

I lifted her from the wheelchair and sat her in the massage chair. I put the money into the slot and the chair began to vibrate. My Granny's eyes were as big as 50-cent pieces. I laughed! She looked at me as only she could! I changed the setting and her eyes became normal. She relaxed and began to

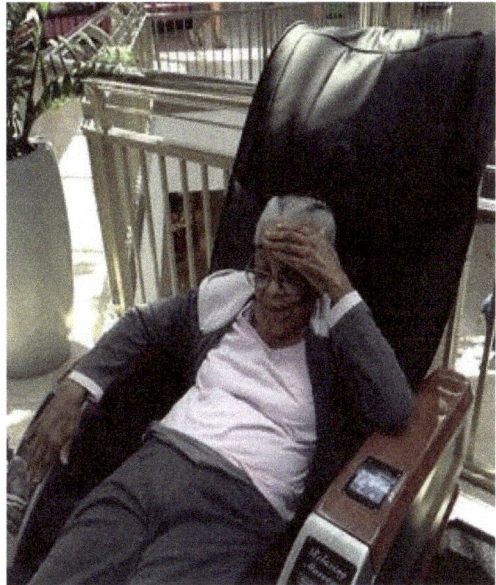

watch the people passing by.

Just as she began to blink her eyes trying to fight sleep, the massage ended.

"You wanna do it some more Granny?" I asked. "No ma'am. I wanna eat," she said. That admission as music to my ears because her appetite had been challenged. I took her out of the chair, put her back in the wheelchair and made our way to the food court.

After much deliberation, she chose nuggets and fries from Chick-Fil-A and a smoothie from Orange Julius.

We made it back to the car. After she was settled and I put the wheelchair into the car, I got in the driver's seat. "Thank you so much for a beautiful day," Granny said. I smiled and thought, "This was the best day EVER."

The turnaround was amazing! She went from barely eating to asking for seconds at every meal. She went from staying in the bed all day to asking to put on clothes and requesting to sit outside on the porch for a little while every day.

I tried to schedule regular days out that didn't involve going to the doctor.

On one of those days, we went to the hair salon and to the nail salon. She had a ball! She posed for the pictures at the end of the day. That night, she slept like a baby

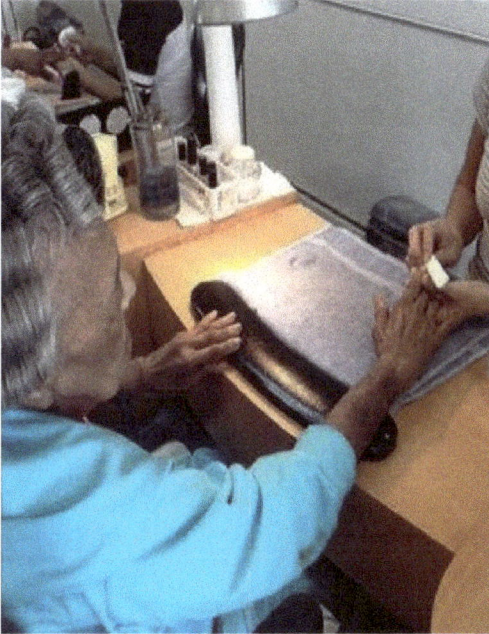

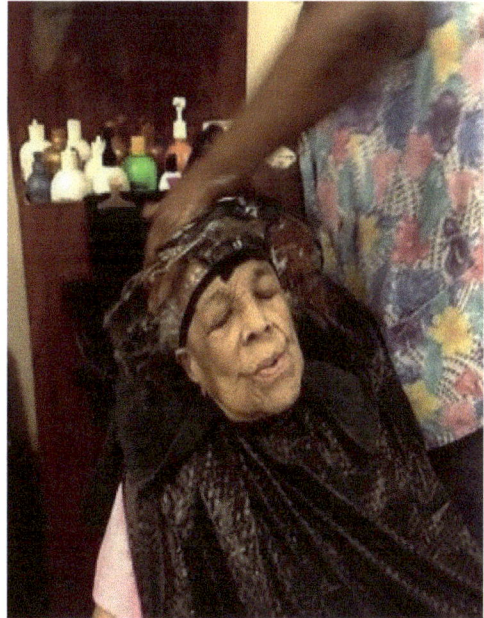

I truly enjoyed that summer with my Granny and contemplated not going back to North Carolina so I could continue helping my momma care for my Granny, but I knew my assignment wasn't finished.

I traveled back very reluctantly. Within a few days, my Granny's condition began to decline again.

Chapter 15

Losing My Granny

I didn't want to leave to go back to North Carolina, but I had to go back to work. Quitting was an option that I was strongly considering though. The only semblance of consolation that I had was the improvements that my Granny was experiencing. She was eating more, talking more, and even smiling more.

Within a few days of my return to North Carolina, that all changed. My Granny became bed bound again. She stopped talking again, and her appetite waned. I quickly made my way back to Georgia.

My Granny was admitted into the hospital. It was as if I was admitted, too, because I was there from sunup to sundown, watching, praying, decreeing and declaring, watching the doctors intensely, and rebuking the devil.

We'd been in times of her health declining before, but this felt different.

My Granny told us before this decline that she was gonna be here longer. "I'm gonna make it to 100, but after that, we'll have to talk about it," Granny said. She was 92, so I was determined to fight for her next eight years.

I walked into my Grandma's hospital room. Nurses were working and my Granny was unconscious. She was on a ventilator. My heart sank.

The days with her on the ventilator felt like they lasted forever. The doctors began to say things that were very discouraging. We were, eventually, presented with the tough decision of taking her off the ventilator.

We gathered in my Granny's room -- my mom, my sister, two aunts, cousins, and my grandma's pastor. The nurse removed the ventilator and we prayed.

I still believed that God could and would heal my Granny.

She was moved to another room, out of the ICU.

One night, she had a seizure. The nurses rushed into the room and began to work on her. They yelled at me asking if they should help her or just let her go.

"What? How did we get here? Just a few weeks ago, she was laughing, smiling, and talking. Now, I'm being asked to decide if she would live or die." My thoughts raced as panic flooded my heart.

"YESSS!" I yelled back as the nurses attached equipment to my Granny! They stabilized her.

The next four days were so scary.

On October 12, 2015, my Granny took her last breath as my sister and I surrounded her bed. I prayed the prayer of resurrection, as my sister stood in agreement with me. I started to cry. "Don't give up! Keep praying," my sister said.

Granny decided that she was ready to go.

My sister being the pillar of strength, as always, comforted the crying nurse, and helped to prepare my Granny's remains for the morgue.

My life changed yet again. My best friend was gone.

Chapter 16

Losing My Momma

My momma took my Granny's passing very hard. She was sad most of the time.

She had this persistent cough, caused by chronic obstructive pulmonary disease (COPD), that seemed to get worse. Before Granny passed away, she kept encouraging my momma to get that cough checked. My momma thought it was just the COPD, so she didn't pursue it.

She, eventually, decided to get her cough checked. The diagnosis showed that it was as a result of developing lung cancer.

My aunt became her caregiver and I traveled home every other weekend to help. My sister put in for a leave of absence and came home to help, as well.

My mom became even more withdrawn. She started planning, as if she was preparing to die. She asked my aunt to invite her former clients over for an early birthday party because she didn't believe she'd make it to her birthday.

Her health declined quickly.

She went back into the hospital. I stayed every day and night. Her days were good and bad but mostly bad. She talked even less, only short phrases expressing her needs. "I need to pee," and her last words, "I want to go home." I asked whether or not she meant home to 711 Albany Avenue. She, with apparent struggle, said "yes." So, I called my aunt and my sister. I, then, called for the doctors to come to the room. I told them her wishes, and they began to make arrangements to release her to go home.

They cleaned her up, and then we waited for the EMTs to pick us up to transport us home by way of an ambulance.

The walk from the hospital room to the ambulance was a long distance. My mom's eyes were closed. My eyes were wide open. The reality of the moment hit me, and I began to cry as we got closer to the ambulance.

I wasn't allowed to ride in the back with her, which broke my heart even more. I talked to her through the grate that separated the front of the ambulance from the back.

We arrived at home and they placed her in the hospital bed in which my Granny had spent many days, only six months prior.

She had a very close friend, Sarah, who came over to visit that night. On April 30, 2016, my mom took her last breath.

Sarah walked out of the house unable to speak, unable to cry.

I called the hospice nurse. She came over after midnight and confirmed my mom's death and put the date of May 1, 2016, (my Granny's birthday) on the death certificate.

My sister and one of her friends prepared my mom's remains for the morticians to pick her up.

My life changed yet again.

Mentoring Moment (I. Invest)

Invest means to furnish with power, authority, rank, etc. I didn't know my power when I'd succumb to depression. I thought, "it's just a part of me. So, I've just gotta accept it and deal with it." I felt powerless and as if there was nothing I could do about it. I was so wrong! After evaluating and dismantling depression, I had to invest or replenish and restore "my house" (me) with proper furniture and equipment. I spent time combing through the scriptures.

During this phase, it is so important to know your power, authority and rank. The Bible is chocked FULL of scriptures that make clear God's intention for the believer to know, have access to and use our inherited rights. Here are just a few of those scriptures:

Power
19 Behold, I give unto you power to tread on serpents and scorpions, and over all the power of the enemy: and nothing shall by any means hurt you (Luke 10:19, KJV).

Authority
No weapon formed against you shall prosper, And every tongue which rises against you in judgment, You shall condemn (Isaiah 54:17, NKJV).

Rank
"You have made them to be a kingdom and priests to our God; and they will reign upon the earth" (Revelation 5:10, AMP).

Turn to page 20 of your H.O.W. Workbook and begin PHASE 3, Invest.

Chapter 17

Something Is Wrong

The end of the school day had come. I walked my students to the bus parking lot, as normal. I was walking back to my classroom when I saw a parent of one of my former students. "Hey, Ms. Usry," she very excitedly said. "Hey," I replied. She moved closer to me looking intensely at my face. "You okay?" she questioned. "Yeah. I'm just tired."

"You look a little more than tired."

"I'm okay." She didn't believe me. She started telling me about a homeopathic doctor and she encouraged me to go see him. She said she would contact the doctor immediately to tell him about me. I assured her that I would call.

Every Wednesday, we'd take a picture as a staff, along with the students whose parents were on the staff. We all wore the color red to support education, "Red for Ed." Just as the curious parent was leaving, the staff began to come from everywhere to take this picture. Questions came from every side, "You okay? Can you drive? Do you need to sit down?" I tried to reassure everyone that I was okay. They didn't believe me. They found a chair, put it in the hallway and insisted that I sit while they surrounded me to take the picture.

After the picture was taken, two of my co-workers informed me that I wouldn't be driving home but one of them would drive to my apartment and the other one would drive my car. Something is wrong!

I started feeling like I wanted my momma and my grandmama. They were both deceased by this time, so I knew I really needed some help.

I called my co-worker, Ebonye, to come, get me and take me to the hospital's Emergency Room. She was there in no time and stayed with me until I was admitted into the hospital. It got really "real!"

One of the parents of two of my former students, Veronica Darrow, became more like a sister to me and I shared everything with her. She is VERY knowledgeable concerning all things medical and natural herbs to assist with healing. She shared her wisdom and knowledge with me during this time and even selflessly carried me to and attended doctor's appointments and lab tests with me.

The wonderful librarian at my school, Valerie Souchek, also helped me in so many ways. One day, she took me to the doctor for a brain MRI, and she cooked and brought food when I was unable to cook for myself.

The mother of my godchildren, Priscilla Yelverton, the chef, prepared meals, as well. They were absolutely amazing.

All of my friends and loved ones knew something was wrong.

Chapter 18

My New Norm

I opened my eyes unsure of what this day would hold. Rising for the day was not the same. It required much effort. I grabbed the bed to try to pull myself up. After about two minutes of tugging and pulling on my disheveled sheets, I was able to sit partially upright in the bed. I, now, had to make it out of the bed and to the bathroom. "Whew!" I thought. This was not my life before. Getting out of bed was never a challenge. Walking? Why is walking so hard? I hardly had any balance. I held onto the dresser, to the bed, to the walls, to whatever sturdy item was available to help get me to my destination.

Now, I had to wake up hours before I needed to depart because everything took much longer to do. I used to be able to wake up, shower, brush my teeth, brush my hair, get dressed, grab something to eat and take Sasha out, all in an hour. Not anymore.

I was late to work every day. I didn't fix my lunch. I interacted with my students less. Adjusting to my "new norm" was not happening. I was, in my opinion, failing miserably.

There was love shown from so many sources during this time! My co-worker, Ebonye, decided to create a GoFundMe campaign to help with my medical bills that were piling up. She had the help of two of our other co-workers, Karen Cromwell and Valerie. They checked on me daily and encouraged others to give to the fund.

Parents of my current students and even my former students gave to the fund. There were too many people to name who gave. I even had two anonymous donors give me $4,000 each. There was over $12,000 raised that put a significant dent in my medical bills.

My god sister, Renee Harrington, who was the Data Manager at my school, made sure that my classroom duty was covered with good substitute teachers. She also made sure that I had donated leave time when mine was exhausted.

My assistant, Linnie James, was absolutely amazing. She handled the classroom and told me not to worry.

My Kindergarten team handled things in my absence, as well. They completed tasks that I could not.

My "new norm" now included people caring for me in very marked and pronounced ways!

Mentoring Moment (F. Fortify)

Fortify means to furnish with a means of resisting force or standing strain or wear. In other words, you must make yourself strong and sturdy. You will build resistance against what previously took up unresisted residence in your house (you).

I began to confess the opposite of the challenging thoughts and suggestions of the enemy because I knew the devil is a liar. Whatever he said to me, the opposite was true because I knew he was incapable of telling the truth. This was helpful when I couldn't remember a scripture appropriate for that particular challenge. Here are a few scriptures that helped and continue to help me fortify:

Neither give place to the devil. (Ephesians 4:27)

Get thee behind me, Satan: for thou savourest not the things that be of God, but the things that be of men. (Mark 8:33)

For the weapons of our warfare are not carnal, but mighty through God to the pulling down of strong holds; Casting down imaginations, and every high thing that exalteth itself against the knowledge of God and bringing into captivity every thought to the obedience of Christ. (2 Corinthians 10:4,5)

Turn to page 22 of your H.O.W. Workbook and begin PHASE 4, Fortify.

Chapter 19

You Do Reap What You Sow

I called my best friend. "I may need you to come and plan to stay for a little while. I need your help."

"No problem," she said. Crystal made plans and arrived at my doorstep a few days later.

My condition continued to decline and I became more dependent. Crystal had to help me out of bed, help me to the bathroom, pick up food, or prepare food for me to eat, pick up meds, wash my clothes, everything because I could basically do nothing on my own.

She cared for me for three weeks. During that time, my sister came home from Dijbouti, Africa for a brief R&R. She helped with my care for a few days until she had to leave to make her way back to Africa.

My aunt traveled from Augusta and helped Crystal with my care. Singularly, my aunt decided that there was no reason for me to remain in North Carolina as I waited for a doctor's appointment that was months away.

Crystal went back to Virginia, and my aunt and I traveled back to Georgia.

My aunt put me in her bedroom, which was previously my Granny's bedroom, and it became my momma's room when she became ill. That room represented the step before the end, in my mind. My granddaddy and my momma both died in that room, and my Granny declined in that room before she died.
My outlook was bleak.

My aunt did the things for me that I'd done for my father, grandfather, grandmother, and mother. She cooked, prepared, or garnered all of my meals. She took me to and from the bathroom. She took me to the doctor. She researched foods to assist with my care. She helped me make decisions concerning my medical care, my living arrangements, and my next step as a teacher. She encouraged me daily and gave me communion. She prayed for and with me and encouraged transformation in my atmosphere by changing what shows I watched and even, sometimes, turning the television off.

The scripture is true. You really do reap what you sow.

Chapter 20

Parting Is Such Sweet Sorrow

I walked through the doors of the school. A very familiar place but a very different walk. My left leg dragged across the threshold as I pushed my walker.

The teachers were gathering, as we'd done every year before the students returned, for professional development and planning. Familiar setting. Familiar people. Familiar atmosphere. Very different me.

Ever since I had been in the hospital four months prior, I questioned my ability to return to the classroom. "How can I possibly still teach? I teach kindergarten. I need energy. I need charisma. I need clarity of mind. I need to be able to process information, to assess learning styles, and student needs. I can barely put a sentence together without serious thought," I pondered as I sat in the meeting with my fellow teachers.

After about an hour, we dismissed for a break. I watched as everyone left the room. I waited. I knew that I walked slowly. So, I didn't want to impede anyone's travels. I finally rose to my feet, after some effort, and started making my way to my classroom. I was met in the hallway by my assistant principal. "How you doing?" she asked. "I've been better," I said. "You have, but it's okay. Is there anything I can do to help you?" The problem with that question? I didn't know the answer! I had no idea what I needed. I didn't know what was up ahead.

I did know that I couldn't continue to teach in the state where I resided. I was not at full capacity and I didn't want to be a disservice to my students.

I walked down the hall to my classroom, opened the door and felt sadness. The possibility of leaving my classroom was starting to sink in.

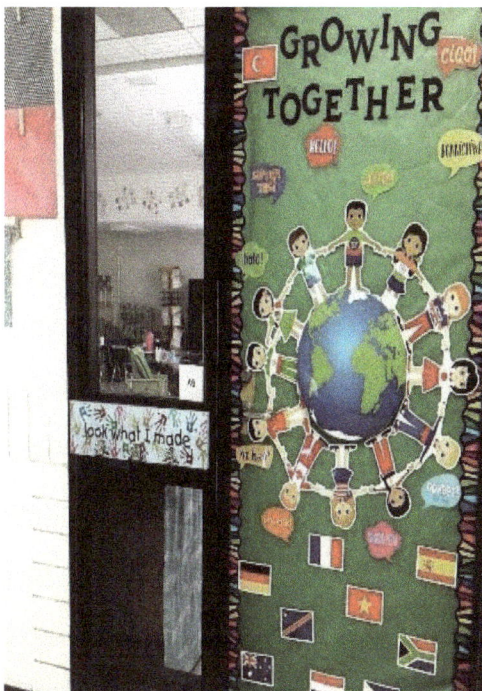

The next day I called my principal. "I'm going to take a leave of absence," I said. He told me the next steps that I needed to take to make this life-altering decision official.

Chapter 21

On the Road Again

I was in Augusta for a few months while still paying rent in North Carolina. My lease wasn't up until the end of February 2020. So, the property manager kept an eye on my sister's car and my apartment. I was basically paying for some expensive storage. No one was living there, just my stuff.

My aunt's pastor, Dr. Robert L. Williams was very instrumental in assisting and caring for my Granny when she was alive. During that last summer, I called on him often for prayer and advisement. I learned to trust him more during that time. So, I asked for his advice on the best way to move all of my belongings. I asked about finding movers and storage that was affordable to pack up all my things, move them to Georgia and store them. A very tall order.

I got some estimates, all astronomical, especially since I was no longer working and had no income.

Pastor Robert asked if I would allow his ministry to assist me with packing and transporting EVERYTHING from my apartment and the school. Three men would do all of this work in just three days. My mind was blown.

I didn't realize all of the stuff that I had until my aunt and Crystal started packing. My friends came to help which included three parents of my former students, "Ketah," Veronica, and "Mia", one of my neighbors, "Ms. T.J.," one of my former church members, Aisha, and my coworker, Ebonye.

We threw away some things and gave away some things.

My aunt strongly encouraged me to throw things away, so did Crystal. We laughed a whole lot and they fussed a whole lot! It was both fun and nerve-wracking.

It ended up requiring two U-Haul trucks and a transporter for my sister's car but Pastor, his team of two men from the church, my friends, my aunt, and my "BFF" got it done. I moved, completely, back home to Augusta, Georgia.

Chapter 22

Back Home Again

I never thought this day would come. Me? Move back to Augusta? No way! I didn't mind visiting but living there was not even a thought.

I always complained that there was not a progressive mindset in the community. Nobody was trying to "come up," trying to do better, trying to have better and I didn't want to be around that kind of thinking.

I would come home to seeing people in the same place mentally, spiritually, financially, and not seeming to want more or better than they have already.

While in North Carolina, I tried numerous avenues to obtain healing. I tried two homeopathic doctors. One of them provided a recommendation to "The Wahl's Protocol" which is a book written by a doctor who has MS. The book provides guidelines for changing your diet. Dr. Wahl's experienced great improvements so I thought I would, too. My aunt began implementing some of the Wahl diet suggestions, to no avail.

The other homeopathic doctor landed me in the hospital. That was not helpful AT ALL!

I tried getting a second opinion because I was not completely satisfied with the first neurologist, so I went to a doctor who practiced through a well-known medical school in Durham. I was given an appointment three months after the date of my request. During this time, my physical condition was beginning to decline.

Once the date finally arrived, the beautiful librarian at my school, Ms. Souchek, took me to my medical appointment.

We were on time but the doctor was not. We waited for almost three hours only to be rushed through the appointment and told it would be three more months before I would even have the conversation about the medication I'd already chosen for treatment. The doctor wanted me to take three months to research the medications that I was already well-versed and fully aware of all there is to know about it.

My aunt decided that there was no need for me to remain in North Carolina for the three-month waiting period. So, she picked me up and brought me home to Georgia.

During this time, my aunt's church began to reach out to us more, praying and asking us if we needed anything.

My aunt shared my challenge regarding long-term care in North Carolina. Her pastor is the founder of Druid Park Community Health Center, a branch of Miracle Making Ministries, which provides healthcare for those in the community who have no health insurance.

The clinic is facilitated through volunteer doctors, nurses, and other medical professionals.

The pastor's wife, Theresa Williams, is one of those volunteers. She began to work diligently to get a referral for me to a highly sought after and recommended doctor in Augusta, Dr. Suzanne Smith.

Dr. Smith's schedule was so filled that her next available appointment was June of the next year.

A nurse practitioner was volunteering at the clinic to get her required level of clinical hours. She learned of Mrs. Williams' endeavors to get a referral for me. "You need a referral? I know her.

I'll get you the referral," she said.

In no time, I received the referral and the appointment was two days before I was scheduled to return to North Carolina for that long-awaited appointment.

Dr. Smith started my care rather quickly! She and her Physician's Assistant, Rebecca Rahn, were very attentive and encouraging.

It was touch and go at the beginning but they worked to help me get some relief in my body.

On my first appointment, I was rolled into the facility bound to a wheelchair. After adding some meds, taking some away, and changing some altogether, the dark days started to have a glimmer of light.

During this time, I also started physical therapy with my wonderful therapist, Terri C. who helped me to improve my mobility!

She treated me like one of her own, not allowing me to be lazy or half-hearted in my therapy.

Dr. Smith and Dr. Rahn learned of my published books during one of my appointments, so we promised to bring them a copy of "Sweet Jambalaya."

The appointment follow-ups were about three months apart after I began to stabilize. We, somehow, kept forgetting to take the book there with us but we finally remembered.

My sister was back home from Djibouti so she took me to my appointment that day. We left the books in the car. So, when the appointment was over, I walked to the front desk to pay the bill and my sister went to get the books out of the car. When she returned, she went back into the exam area to take Dr. Smith the book and she walked back to the front where I was sitting waiting.

"Wow!" Dr. Smith loudly said. Everybody began to look around including my sister who was in midstride headed towards the front where I was waiting.

Dr. Smith emerged from the back of the office with the biggest smile on her face, "Ms. Ethel Mitchell is your grandma?" she questioned as she looked at my granny's picture in the front of the book. "Yes," I said. Dr. Smith exclaimed with great excitement, "She was my patient for over 15 years!"

My jaw dropped. Tajuana sat down. We were both in shock. Dr. Smith cared for our celebrity, which she is to both my sister and me.

"I remember when she was featured in the newspaper. I still have the article," Dr. Smith said. She walked away, went to her office, and came back, moments later with her copy of the article. My Granny was featured in the Augusta Chronicle, on the front page of the Faith section, in 2013, at 90 years old. She was the oldest member of the Path Worship, but she was happy about the congregation and all that she was learning.

"Your grandma was so precious. That explains it. So are you," Dr. Smith extolled.

Many are the plans in a person's heart, but it is the LORD's purpose that prevails. Proverbs 19:21 NIV

I had a plan. God did, too, and His plan always superseded my plan.

Chapter 23

The Fight of My Life

Every day was a struggle. Nothing seemed the same. I didn't want to pray. I didn't want to read scripture. I didn't even want to hear about God.

My wonderful, big sister, Tajuana, texted me every day. She'd encourage and fuss, when needed. "How you gone boss me around from Africa?" I thought but I loved every moment of it! She probably doesn't know how much she encouraged my heart!

My precious Aunt Donaval, who was my caregiver, came into the room every morning, reading scriptural confessions to me, having me repeat them and then she'd read a scripture and ask me what it meant to me and for me. I obeyed and followed the routine, but I loathed it with every fiber of my being. I was in a very dark place, the darkest I'd ever been in my life!

My aunt would also bring me Holy Communion. "Why bother?" I thought. "God doesn't exist. God isn't real. How could He possibly be real? I'd served Him wholeheartedly for over 20 years. How could He let this happen to me? How could He do this to me? Am I being punished?"

My "AA," Crystal, came to Georgia to help care for me. She waited on me hand and foot just like she did in North Carolina. She slept right by my side so she'd be available at all times.

I was having trouble sleeping so I'd often take Benadryl. The huge bottle of little pink pills rested on the nightstand beside the bed. One night, I heard in my thoughts, "You can just go ahead and take a handful of those pills and it will be all over." I turned to Crystal, told her what I had heard, and asked her to remove the pills. She did. At that point, I knew I had to fight, with everything within me.

Prior thoughts of suicide left me when I was 18. I couldn't let them return and take up residence again.

I took the written confessions and began to read them myself. I recorded myself reading them for the days that I didn't feel like reading. I started watching Christian television, especially Joseph Prince because I knew he focused a lot on healing through the communion. I listened to "soaking music" which is what we call music that is soft, soothing, and scripturebased, designed to lead the hearer into the presence of God. I started to pray again, asking God to prove to me that He's real and that He loved me. I asked for our relationship to be restored and to be better than it was before.

He heard me and He honored my request.

Chapter 24

The Black 'N White Chronicles

One of the avenues that God used to restore me was the "Black 'N White Chronicles." I would share an encouraging, quick thought on social media before I got sick. Listeners responded well and loved them, but after the health challenge occurred, I had no desire to say anything to anybody. I felt like I couldn't encourage anybody. I needed encouragement myself.

My aunt would urge me to continue producing them and I would but not without angst. It was a struggle to think of anything encouraging to say about a God in whom I no longer believed.

After the suicide thought, I became determined to share, just in case someone hearing my voice needed encouragement to turn away from taking his own life. The "Chronicles" became more frequent and more and more people began to share how impacted they were by my posts.

I, again, overcame the enemy. If you want to hear and see some of my "Black 'N White Chronicles," I invite you to visit my YouTube page at https://youtu.be/3chudRvxLKU.

Chapter 25

Pathway to Healing

Research is key to understanding any medical problem. So, I researched, and I researched, and I researched. Everything that I saw talked about how MS was terminal and incurable, which as you might imagine, is very discouraging.

My sister, Tajuana, wanted to help my aunt. So, she found a home healthcare company for me, while she was in Djibouti, Africa. She insisted on paying the bill.

The company sent people to help me to get a shower, get dressed, and eat every day. They also helped to clean the bedroom and bathroom where I was spending most of my time.

My aunt, very unselfishly, allowed me to use her bedroom and so much more. Her sacrifices were endless.

During this time, I met some good caregivers. They offered something unique and encouraging. They made me laugh, encouraged me through scriptures or prayer, or affirmations.

My aunt inspired me every day by reading affirmations and having me repeat them. She read me a Bible verse and asked questions that provoked me to think. She encouraged me to turn off the TV and to be careful about the genre of music to which I listened. On some days, she prayed with me which is what I needed because I, at one point, had no desire to pray. She also encouraged me to post on social media. I was asked almost every day if I'd posted a "Black 'N White Chronicles." She thought that others would be encouraged as they watched my journey.

As a result, I received an inbox message on Instagram from a woman whom I'd met some years prior, but we didn't really talk to each other at that time. Her message was written as follows:

"Good morning, woman of God!! I remember meeting you years ago at a funeral where you preached in Augusta, Georgia! Oh, the anointing .... I don't want to get into your personal space, but I read a post of yours that said MS was your diagnosis. I'd be crazy not to share this with you.

"My husband was diagnosed with Remitting Relapsing MS in July 2019. The neurologist in Savannah did all tests to confirm three lesions on his brain. They wanted to start him on medication right away. The first medication they wanted to try was intended to make his heart rate go so low that he would have to be monitored for the first twelve hours. We prayed and got confirmation to get another opinion for treatment. Medical docs won't tell us but there are ways to help the body heal itself without strong medication. We were introduced to Dr. Aaron Ernst of askdrernst.com. Please look him up. My husband's cousin works in his Charlotte, North Carolina office. He is a holistic chiropractor who specializes in treating MS and all types of autoimmune illnesses.

"If you want more information, please reach out to me. I will be happy to share some of the food protocol and supplement names that he takes. Either way, I'll continue to pray and believe God for your and my husband's complete healing."

This message caught my attention immediately! I started thinking about the cost at the same time. I was no longer working, so I had no income. I'd heard about holistic doctors before. I'd even tried one a few months before that landed me in the hospital for three days earlier that year. So, there were all kinds of barriers going on in my heart and mind. This option felt like an avenue that was unexplorable, but I knew I had to try something else. The strong medication, "Ocrevus," scared me. My condition was declining. I needed direction and help from God, DESPERATELY!

I called Dr. Ernst for a consultation. I was made aware of all that this process would entail, and I had to make a decision.

The first part of the process required three tests that were expensive. That made me nervous, but I wanted a different method of treatment.

Lady Golanda arranged a time when I could talk to her and her husband and ask them any questions about Dr. Ernst and his treatment plans.

Sean, Golanda's husband, with a voice that sounded similar to my daddy's, was very personable and helpful. I was thinking, "Wow! These are cool people and very helpful. I hope they won't feel like I wasted their time when they find out I can't afford it."

That thought went on for the duration of the conversation until the end. "The initial tests are expensive but they are worth the expense and if you decide to do it, Sean and I will sow those tests into your life. We'll pay for them."

My mouth dropped as gratitude flooded my heart! God was honoring my request.

I took the test, had a consult with Dr. Ernst, and decided to start the protocol that he suggested.

I saw marked improvements on the first day of treatment and the improvements continued.

My diet changed completely which was totally plausible because there are a ton of recipes on Dr. Ernst's website. I eat clean food and that has made a world of difference. I also take supplements specific to what my body needs, which was discovered from the initial test.

Dr. Ernst is a godsend and I'd recommend him to any and everyone. Working with him will change your life. It definitely changed mine.

Chapter 26

She's Ba-a-a-ack

I had to overcome so much.

I couldn't walk. Now, I'm walking. I didn't want to pray anymore. Now, I'm praying. I didn't want to read the Bible, so I didn't. Now, I want to read again and I'm reading. I didn't talk on the phone. Now, I'm talking on the phone again. I wasn't writing. Now, I'm writing again. I wrote and performed poetry. I hadn't done that in a while. I stopped making plans for my future. I've written out a five-year plan and I've started implementing things already to accomplish those goals. I'm following the E.D.I.F.Y. phases to accomplish each goal!

In summation, "SHE'S BA-A-A-ACK!" I can now show and tell you H.O.W.!

Mentoring Moment (Y. Yield)

Yield means to produce or furnish. During this last phase of transformation, you produce, furnish, or supply the things that you were previously hindered from doing. For example, when I was challenged with depression, I couldn't function around others. I was closed off, sad, isolated even in the presence of others. Once I overcame, I became the life of the party. I made others laugh. I offered insight, wisdom, prayer, and just my presence which often helped others to overcome their challenges and accomplish their goals. ***Turn to page 24 of your H.O.W. Workbook and begin PHASE 5, the final phase, Yield.***

Chapter 27

Welcomed Letters of the Alphabet H.O.W.

So, now what? Now, you win, and you keep on winning!

I was listening to and watching my half-brother, A.J., via Facebook Live. He exhorted the congregation, Divine Unity Christian Church (DUCC), where he is blessed to be the executive pastor. This was a Sunday morning during the Novel Coronavirus Disease (COVID19) pandemic.

He encouraged the church family to lift their voices in praise to God. During this time, he recalled the story of the walls of Jericho in the Bible (Joshua 6). I'd heard the story many times so I was awaiting the common train of thought that would come from the preacher's mind and out of his or her mouth. "The walls came down because of the army's obedience. We must praise God so the walls in our lives will come tumbling down." I'd heard these thoughts a thousand times.

He encouraged praise and then he began to talk about the rubble that resulted from the walls coming down. He said that it is proposed that the rubble became a bridge for the people to get into the city. WHAT???? I'd never heard that before? What was once a barrier, became a ramp or bridge to help them get into the once fortified city.

This biblical story provoked me to further study. The soldiers were instructed to walk around the city of Jericho, once a day for six days, but on the seventh day they were instructed to walk around the city seven times. Seven times in one day, the last day before the wall came down.

The walls were an estimated 12-17 feet high, 5-6 feet thick and the distance around the city was approximately 2,000 feet. Can you picture it? I can! This barrier was huge, and massive, and had to appear to be impossible to overtake. How could they get through this massive, fortified, expansive barrier? What emotions, sensations, bodily responses did this experience produce? Did water taste the same under this extreme expenditure of energy? Was there a new level of muscle aches and pains? What did it smell like? What were they hearing? What changed? What remained the same? What did that feel like? What?

I, immediately, thought about MS, a fortified wall, a barrier against which I've been destined, created to achieve. Everything changed. Nothing remained the same. Food didn't even taste the same. I couldn't see as well as before. I couldn't walk as well as I once did. I couldn't interpret sensations because I couldn't feel things. I had numbness in my appendages. All of these things and more seemed to have been a permanent lifelong obstruction that could never be moved. I was sure that these Jericho walls were there because I was being punished for some past sin or sins. How can this possibly "work together for my good?"

I began to look at all of the things that happened since this health challenge began. My faith grew because my time with God grew. I was at home and in a constant state most of the time. I heard God more.

I've written and published three books since the start of my health challenge with the plan for publishing seven more books. I hadn't published a book in the previous two years.

I've created a business to mentor others with these proven principles of overcoming Satan's roadblocks. I've attended to my mental health by seeing a therapist, Dr. Faye. My credit worthiness has been restored and my student loans have been completely wiped out. I've been able to write out my life plan for the next five years and I've already accomplished some of the goals that I had set for myself. God gets ALL the glory!

MS was my fortified wall that miraculously came down and became the rubble that I walked upon to enter into the place of my destiny!

My perception has changed forever! I no longer see trials, challenges, and hard places as immovable fortresses that guarantee my failure or deny me access. They are the opposite! They have become rubble at the sound of my voice and ramps onto which I climb to accomplish my goals.

The same can be true for you! You have gone through the necessary steps to overcome every challenge and setting goals. You are an overcomer! Now, WIN!

Change your perception of barriers standing in your way and transform your life, FOREVER! Now, go and E.D.I.F.Y. someone else because you now know **H.O.W.**!

The Author

(Photo courtesy of Walter Jennette of Feelm Studios)

Tralyne DeShea Usry was born on May 11, 1976, in

Augusta, Georgia. She is the daughter of the late Mrs. Karen M. Dyers and the late Mr. Jimmy L. Usry. She is the granddaughter of the late Mr. Joseph W. Mitchell and the late Mrs. Ethel A. Mitchell. She is also the surrogate daughter of her aunt, Ms. Donaval J. Mitchell, who has been instrumental in every facet of her life from birth to now. She has many siblings but shares a close relationship with her sister, Tajuana D. Usry, a historymaking Gunners Mate for the United States Coast Guard.

Tralyne attended undergraduate school at Paine College in Augusta, where she graduated with a Bachelor of Arts degree in Communication, with an emphasis in print journalism. She studied Directing for Film and Television at Regent University in Virginia Beach, Virginia. She also studied and received a Master of Science degree in Education from Ashford

University in Clinton, Iowa.

She was taught in the admonition of God at one of the oldest churches in Augusta, Georgia -- Thankful Baptist Church. However, she did not accept Jesus Christ as her Savior until she was 18 years old on March 3, 1995, at 2:30 AM. This transformation happened during a shut-in under the leadership of Prophetess Juanita Bynum-Weeks of Waycross, Georgia.

She was further nurtured and brought into sonship (maturity) at the Word Is Life Church where she received her Minister's License in 1997 under the leadership of Apostle Aline and Pastor Martrice Scott.

Upon moving to Virginia Beach to attend Regent University, God began to funnel into her a new anointing to write and perform poetry. Since then, she has written a book, "**Aesthetically, Audibly Me**," that is a collection of poetry and spoken word pieces designed to point the reader, through visual images, and audible sounds, to the person and work of Jesus Christ!

She wrote a second poetry book, "**When Design Speaks**," which contains poetry and spoken word pieces also but the focus is on the reader becoming whomever God has designed them to be!

Tralyne was also fortunate to participate in a contest which resulted in her being named Hampton Roads Rising Gospel Artist in 2004.

After winning the contest, she appeared on the "Bobby Jones New Artist Showcase" which was televised on the WORD Network on September 18, 2004.

She was also featured in the first-ever <u>Essence Hot Hair Magazine</u>, October 2010, as well as three subsequent black hair magazines, as a feature model for Shawn's Hair & More, Richmond, Virginia.

She was a member of the Greater Touch of Compassion

Ministries, Richmond, Virginia under the leadership of Apostle Ezreaonne Jackson for nine years, where she very excitedly served as a Board Member, Armor Bearer, Youth Director, member of the Voices of Compassion Praise and Worship team, member of the Finance Team, Director and Choreographer of Expressed Glory (a liturgical dance team) and Director of the Worship in Arts Ministry. In August of 2012, the Lord called her supervising Apostle back to California, and Greater Touch was dissolved.

Teaching has always been Tralyne's passion. She has been afforded the privilege of teaching various age groups. Her first teaching experience with the first grade at Christian Hope School in Woodbridge, Virginia catalyzed for her to continue in education. She went on to teach preschool at Victory Christian Academy in Richmond, Virginia. She taught kindergarten, her favorite grade, at Southwest Elementary School, Durham, North Carolina.

After an encounter at a Women's Conference, Dr. Sharon Nesbitt, Apostle and Founder of Dominion Outreach Ministries, Marion, Alaska, spoke the Word of the Lord over her life, laid hands, and Elder Tralyne received activation of the gift of the prophetic. She now moves with accuracy and precision, hearing and seeing the will of the Lord for His people. This encounter also activated the courage to answer the call to launch Infuse Dominion International Outreach Ministries, an organization geared to share the message of the kingdom with those that have been deemed unreachable and unwanted. Through this ministry and partnership with Miracle Making Ministries, she has successfully hosted Agape' Village Summer Reading and Performing Arts Summer Camps, for the past four years, which serves students from kindergarten through fifth grades, focusing on reading remediation, and strengthening literacy skills. The students were also taught different performing arts skills. The camp ended each year with a performance by the students showcasing what they have learned during the course of the camp. This performance was attended by the local community and others from far and near.

Tralyne has been blessed with the opportunity to minister on various denominational and non-denominational platforms. Her passion for God and the desire to see others experience His love is phenomenal and promises to change your life. She served in the five-fold ministry office of a teacher with prophetic insight and apostolic commissioning.

She published her second book which was geared towards children called, **"Sweet Jambalaya**." This story championed the causes of "Puey" the Skunk, "Tybe" the Caterpillar, "Katey" the Lady Bug, and "Sammy" the Squirrel, all of whom varied in their ethnicity, and physical appearances making them typical targets for bullies. They learned through acceptance and affirmation how to overcome the bullies that attacked them from without and within!

She was nominated as "Author of The Year/Social Awareness" for **Sweet Jambalaya** by the Indie Author Legacy Awards. She was also named as a finalist, selected from over 800 authors.

She has written more books: "Nebby," her second children's book and an "Amazon Best-Seller." In her latest book release, "H.O.W.," which also has a helpful companion workbook, she details her memoirs of challenges that she has faced and overcome in her life.

www.ingramcontent.com/pod-product-compliance
Lightning Source LLC
Chambersburg PA
CBHW061407090426
42739CB00020B/3494